Lt.-Col. F. W. E. JOHNSON, D.S.O., to whose gallant leadership and untiring energy the Battalion owes much in the field of War and of Sport.

A SHORT RECORD

OF THE

SERVICES AND EXPERIENCES

OF THE

5th Battalion Royal Irish Fusiliers,

IN THE

GREAT WAR.

TO THE MEMORY OF

THE

Officers, Non-Commissioned Officers and Men

OF THE

5th & 6th (Service) Battalions, Royal Irish Fusiliers,

WHO FELL ON THE FIELD OF BATTLE.

FOREWORD.

I have been asked to write a foreword to this little book, and do so gladly, as it gives me an opportunity of expressing my unbounded admiration for the Officers, N.C.O's. and men who, during the period of the war, have formed the Battalion.

Having been with the unit from its earliest days till now, except for a short period in hospital, I feel that I am in a position fully to realise all the hardships, so cheerfully and uncomplainingly borne, of GALLIPOLI, SERBIA, MACEDONIA, PALESTINE and FRANCE, and the magnificent efforts made to overcome the enemy, wherever met. The *esprit de corps* of the Battalion has at all times been very great, and the honour of the Regiment has been worthily maintained.

Many incidents of interest and accounts of gallant deeds have necessarily been omitted by reason of the brevity of the book.

I wish to express my grateful thanks to the Editors. Their task has been no small one, as it has been done on Active Service, and with practically no records to which reference might be made.

In conclusion, I wish all members of the Battalion, both past and present, "GOD SPEED," and I assure them that I shall never forget the great honour that has fallen to my lot—the command of the 5th Royal Irish Fusiliers for nearly two years.

F. W. E. JOHNSON, *Lieut.-Col.*

January, 1919.

RECORD

OF

5th Battalion Royal Irish Fusiliers, 1914-1918.

CHAPTER I.

TRAINING DAYS.

Almost immediately after the declaration of hostilities that inaugurated The Great War, a call went forth from Lord Kitchener for one hundred thousand volunteers to form a New Army. This new formation comprised six Divisions, numbering from the 9th to the 14th. Ireland's contribution came to be known as the 10th (Irish) Division.

On the 10th August, 1914, orders were received to form the 5th and 6th Service Battalions of the Royal Irish Fusiliers as part of this Division. Within the next fortnight some two hundred men joined the Colours at ARMAGH, and the following Officers were posted to the 5th Battalion:—Capt. F. W. E. Johnson, Lieut. P. E. Kelly, Lieut. E. M. MacIlwaine, and Lieut. W. Stewart.

On the 24th August the Battalion moved to Portobello Barracks, Dublin, and was joined by Lieut. J. Campbell, who was appointed Quartermaster. Soon after arrival at Portobello Barracks, Lieut. Col. G. H. J. Rooke, of the Leinster Regiment, was appointed to command, and joined the Battalion.

Recruits arrived in a steady stream, till by the 10th September the Battalion reached the approximate strength of 700. Orders were then received to transfer some 400 N.C.O's. and men to form the nucleus of the 6th Battalion, and Lieut. Col. F. A. Greer was appointed to command it. Recruits still poured in, and by the end of September the Battalion was about 1,400 strong. About this time 500 of these men were drafted to TIPPERARY, under the command of Col. R. S. H. Moody, to form the nucleus of the

7th Battalion. During this time training was being carried out under considerable difficulties; equipment was slow in coming; experienced Officers and N.C.O's. were few, and these had the heavy task of training the new Officers and N.C.O's. at the same time as the large numbers of men.

However, about the middle of October, training and equipping were really in full swing, and the men already began to do justice to their instructors. There is little to record between now and Christmas, when a well-merited leave was granted to all ranks. About this time the Commanding Officer underwent an operation, after which he was passed medically unfit; Major M. J. W. Pike being appointed Lieut.-Col. to command the Battalion.

In spite of the strenuousness of the work and training, sports of all sorts were not lost sight of, and there were some very keen struggles between the various Battalions in the Brigade (31st Bde., composed of 5th and 6th R. Innis. Fus. and 5th and 6th R. Irish Fus.), in which the Battalion set a standard of " Second to None " which they maintained in all the formations to which they later belonged throughout the War.

By Christmas all preliminary training had been completed, and it may here be noted that the Battalion had very creditable results in Musketry on the Dollymount Ranges, despite the fact that it was often carried out when snow lay deep upon the ground. After a return from Leave about the middle of January the more advanced stages of training were entered upon, and by the end of February the Battalion was quite fit to take its place in the Brigade and Divisional exercises.

About this time the Battalion was inspected by the Inspector-General of Infantry—Major-General Vesey Dawson, who expressed himself as well pleased with the progress in equipment and training. Towards the end of February the Battalion took its place in lining the streets of DUBLIN on the departure of the retiring Viceroy of Ireland, Lord Aberdeen, and a few days later at the entry of his successor, Lord Wimborne. The steadiness of the Battalion at this, its first ceremonial parade, was very noticeable.

The military situation permitting, a whole holiday was granted for Barrosa Day, which was celebrated according to the time-honoured custom of the Regiment. Athletic sports were held, and one of the chief features was an Officers' Relay Race open to the

Brigade, which was easily won by the Battalion. In the evening the Officers entertained a large number of guests, the chief amongst them being Brigadier-General F. F. Hill, C.B., Commanding 31st Infantry Brigade, representatives from practically all Battalions of the Regiment being present.

Saint Patrick's Day was, of course, a holiday : in the morning there was a parade for the distribution of Shamrocks presented to the Battalion, and thereafter the Day was celebrated in noble style.

Towards the end of March, Brigade and Divisional training took place, marking a step further in the advance of the Battalion for active operations. About the middle of April the Brigade was reviewed in PHŒNIX PARK by His Excellency the Lord Lieutenant, the Battalion being again noticeable for its steadiness on parade and the excellence of turn-out.

Rumour of a move now began to make itself strongly felt, and many were the destinations prophesied for the Battalion. When it presently transpired that the destination was Basingstoke, great was the disappointment of the fire-eaters who expected to sail across the seas. On arrival at Basingstoke on the 29th April, the Battalion went under canvas, a new experience to many of the Officers, Non-Commissioned Officers and Men. Then came a period of further Divisional training, and opportunity was given to see other Divisions of The First Hundred Thousand at work. During May the Battalion, as part of the Irish Division, was inspected first by Sir Archibald Hunter, General Officer Commanding-in-Chief, Aldershot Command, and later in the month by Lord Kitchener. Both Reviewing Officers expressed satisfaction at the turn-out and soldier-like bearing of the Division. Early in June the Battalion went to Aldershot for Musketry, and whilst there had the honour to march past His Majesty The King in the vicinity of " Cæsar's Camp." His Majesty graciously expressed his approbation of the appearance and bearing of the men.

On the return of the Battalion to Basingstoke, the chief event of interest was a Brigade Sports Meeting, at which the Battalion, gaining premier honours, once more proved its prowess on the Field of Sport. Rumour once more became rife, but on Khaki Drill and " Gippy " Helmets being issued, Gallipoli and Mesopotamia were easily favourites in the betting.

CHAPTER II.

*GALLIPOLI.

On the 11th July the Battalion embarked for Active Service at Devonport on board His Majesty's Transport "ANDANIA." Weather proved favourable, and during an enjoyable voyage Gibraltar, Malta, Alexandria, and later the Ægean Islands of Lemnos and Mitylene were touched at. At Alexandria the men of the Battalion were able to stretch their legs ashore, marching through the town to the strain of the pipes and drums. The Battalion remained at PORT IERO in Mitylene for some days, and on the 3rd August, General Sir Ian Hamilton came aboard to inspect the unit. Whilst here an unfortunate epidemic of European Cholera ran through the Battalion, affecting some 400 men. It had now become evident that the Division had to play a part in the forcing of the Dardanelles.

Speculation naturally ran high as to the probable point of landing, Gallipoli or Asia Minor. On the evening of the 6th August the S.S. "OSMANIEH" came alongside, took aboard the Battalion complete, and set sail in the evening, for a destination still unknown. However, by studying the ship's course, and comparing it with the setting sun and compasses, it became apparent to all that Gallipoli was, indeed, the destination. About one in the morning the watchful were rewarded by seeing gun flashes in the distance. The battle zone was getting closer: soon the decks of the steamer were thronged, and despite strict injunctions to silence it was impossible to suppress the excited murmurings to which all gave vent. Dawn broke and found the ship off Suvla Bay, surrounded by craft of every description—cruisers, destroyers, monitors, motor boats, transports and lighters. Already the battle had begun on the left, the 11th Division being engaged in getting a footing on the shore. As the light improved the warships opened a covering fire with guns of all calibres, to which the enemy made immediate reply by sweeping the beaches with high explosive and shrapnel.

---

*See Map page 40.

On board the " Osmanieh " the final preparations for the struggle were put in train : machine guns were stripped and cleaned, riflebolts were given their final oiling, and many a man ran his finger along his bayonet. But, as on the eve of every battle in history, there were the nonchalant few who continued their card-games.

At last came the order to land. Lighters arrived alongside about 7.0 a.m., and two Companies at a time were taken ashore and landed on " C " Beach under shrapnel fire. The immediate objective was the Northern Slopes of hill LALA BABA, which overlooked " B " Beach. Here a halt was made for some hours to await the landing of further units of the Division. About 11 a.m. the Brigade, with two Companies of the 7th Royal Dublin Fusiliers attached, was in the neighbourhood of LALA BABA, and received orders for the attack. The objective given was YILGIN BURNU (afterwards famous as CHOCOLATE HILL) and GREEN HILL, some three miles distant from the shore. These hills are at the Western end of a chain of heights that overlook the Bay and the ANAFARTA PLAIN. A direct frontal attack was impossible, as the Salt Lake lay between.

The alternative was to make a left flanking movement across the Anafarta Plain, skirting the edge of the Lake. This involved two of the most difficult movements known in warfare, namely, a flank march in the face of the enemy, including the crossing of a considerable obstacle in full view and under the direct fire of the enemy artillery, and a complete change of direction after the attack had been definitely launched.

The attack was opened by the Battalion, with the 6th Royal Inniskilling Fusiliers on the right, two companies of the Dublin Fusiliers in support, and the 6th Battalion of the Regiment in reserve. The advance began by a descent shorewards from the eminence of Lala Baba along the sand dunes of " B " Beach as far as HILL 10. This movement was immediately observed by the enemy, who laid upon the dunes a heavy barrage of high explosive. After passing the shelter of HILL 10 it became necessary to cross the mouth of the Salt Lake where it enters the sea, a morass some sixty yards in breadth, where men sank above the knees. At this point heavy casualties were sustained, for here the enemy concentrated the fire of about twenty of his guns. Shortly after passing this obstacle a change of direction was necessary, and the

Battalion advanced to the attack in an almost due easterly line across the Anafarta Plain. This plain is dead level, but covered with clumps of scrub and gorse, with here and there a tree.

The main Turkish force was on the heights that overlooked the plain, but in the scrub there lurked dozens of snipers, a great many of whom remained silent until the advancing troops had passed them. These then took a heavy toll of such as were conspicuous as leaders, whether they were Officers, N.C.O's. or men. By dusk the plain had been crossed, in spite of the heavy casualties, and the objective was within reach. By 8 p.m. Chocolate Hill had been stormed and captured by representatives of all the Battalions concerned in the attack. Some of the first troops, however, to arrive at the summit of the hill belonged to the Battalion.

That night and the following day were spent in re-organising and consolidating the position captured. About 3 o'clock on the morning of the 9th the Battalion advanced and took up position on Green Hill, which had been occupied the previous day by the South Staffords. At 4.0 a.m. the enemy launched a strong counter-attack, and came up to the assault in a most determined fashion. They were driven off, only to re-organise and come on once more with redoubled effort, but again in vain.

Until the 12th the Battalion remained on Green Hill, subjected to heavy bombardment, but no more counter-attacks had to be met. During all this time the troops suffered greatly from the lack of water : the few wells that were found were subjected to continual sniping, and many men who had bravely volunteered to fill the water bottles of their comrades lost their lives. The great heat of the day, the sand, the flies, the very food—bully and biscuit—all combined to intensify the thirst of the troops.

At 4.0 a.m. on the 12th the Battalion was relieved by the Royal Dublin Fusiliers, and marched back to the beach. Daylight broke before the shelter of Lala Baba had been reached, and a heavy shell-fire was opened on the unit. Respite from the struggle was short, for that same afternoon orders were received to relieve the Lancashire Fusiliers on Karakol Dagh, a high hill some three miles away on the left. About this time dysentry, which in a fortnight had reduced the troops to a state of great weakness, first made its appearance.

On the 14th the Battalion's first reinforcements, three Officers and 200 other ranks, who had been dropped at Mudros in passing, arrived.

On the 15th, the Brigade, in conjunction with part of the 30th Brigade, was ordered to attack Kidney Hill, about a mile eastwards. The Battalion being in reserve was not called upon until 6 o'clock on the morning of the 16th, when it relieved the Royal Dublin Fusiliers on the Pimple, which was enfiladed from the left by eight machine guns, and from the right by artillery fire. All day long the hill was held, in spite of repeated counter-attacks, and the men were often in hand-to-hand conflict with the enemy. The troops on the right having failed to gain their objective, and the right flank of the Division being in the air, a readjustment of the line became necessary. This was carried out in accordance with orders, and at 7.30 p.m. the Battalion proceeded to " A " Beach, where it remained all the following day.

On the 19th the Battalion took over trenches on Green Hill, and entered upon a period of trench warfare which continued until 30th September. The 5th and 6th Battalions of the Regiment during all this period relieved one another, and took part in some local enterprises. During the attack on the 21st, however, the Battalion was in reserve.

By the evening of the 16th the Battalion had been reduced by casualties in the field and by disease to 4 Officers and about 160 other ranks. This remaining number was reduced in health by bad and uncongenial food, scarcity of water and alternate exposure to a burning sun by day and a damp cold by night. Suffering was still further increased by the continual strain of action, lack of proper rest and sleep, and by the very heavy digging that was necessary. Many gallant deeds remain officially unknown on account of the great number of casualties among the Officers and N.C.O's. whose duty it would have been to record them.

The Peninsula of Gallipoli was unique among the battlegrounds of the Great War. It knew no back areas or bases ; in it there was never respite from the strain of active operations : from front line to beach was under enemy domination, and in the daylight hours every movement brought its bombardment from the heights. To this theatre of war, that has been described as possessing each and every military disadvantage, the Battalion bade its adieu on the 30th September, and sailed to the Island of Lemnos to recuperate.

CHAPTER III.

SERBIA.

Lemnos, which was second in discomfort only to Gallipoli, had this advantage, that food and water could be obtained in fair quantities. The period of recuperation was occupied in re-equipping, route marching and Brigade training. At the end of ten days the Battalion, with the remainder of the Division, was warned for a new campaign somewhere in the Balkans. At this time Bulgaria entered the war, and made an attack against the right flank of the Serbian army, virtually stabbing it in the back when it was making its gallant stand against the Austrians.

The Battalion, as part of the Allied Relief Force, landed at Salonica in October, arriving there on the 26th of the month. The Serbian Army at this time was in a precarious position, in danger of breaking in two, and although an Allied Force was at hand to assist it, great delay was caused owing to the fact that only one single line of railway lay between Salonica and Serbia, with a very limited supply of rolling stock at the disposal of the Allied troops.

The Battalion, during its stay on the outskirts of Salonica, was encamped at Lambet, and on the 27th October it entrained for Gjevgjeli, a railhead on the Greek-Serbian Frontier. The situation was still obscure, and a halt was made at Furka, some two days' march from railhead. After a fortnight here the Battalion advanced to Tartali, where it became Brigade Reserve. The heart of the Macedonian mountain system, west of Lake Doiran, had now been reached. The difficulties of transport were colossal; amongst the mountain fastnesses roads were unknown—mere donkey tracks, running in some places almost perpendicularly, had served the purpose of the inhabitants.

About the 20th November the Division was reinforced by the most available troops that could be sent from home, the Battalion receiving some eight Officers and 400 other ranks (very good material) from the Bedfordshire Regiment.

Orders were now received to take over the line at Memisli from the Royal Inniskilling Fusiliers, two Companies occupying a prominent mountain spur, afterwards known as Rocky Peak. The Division was now holding a line of ten miles of mountain country with its Right Flank resting on Lake Doiran, whilst the French were extending west and northwards in an endeavour to gain touch with the Serbs. This was an immense problem, owing to lack of roads and communications, and to the climatic conditions at the time. Hitherto conditions had been fine, and the operations had been carried out in crisp Autumn weather. Now Winter set in fast, rain fell in torrents, only to be succeeded by a thick blizzard of sleet and snow. Coats, blankets and garments of the men were soaked; there was no shelter obtainable on the rock-bound mountains from wind or weather. Then frost set in, making the mountain paths slippery with ice and all but impassable. Coats and blankets which had been soaked froze stiff, and could not be dried. Men huddled together on the lee side of the rocks, which meagre shelter was all that was available. Here were no dugouts, or trenches, in which to obtain a modicum of warmth and protection from the elements, for what ground was not frozen iron hard was a mass of living rock. Frostbite set in under these conditions, and thinned ranks that were not over strong at the best. The work of the stretcher-bearers was exceedingly arduous at this time. To them fell the task of carrying down the mountain slopes the frozen, the wounded and the dead. The transport personnel suffered untold hardship and misery. All loads had to be carried on pack mules, and supplies had to be taken by them at night over uncertain mountain paths where a false step on the frozen ground would very often have meant certain death. Hardened men wept that their numbed fingers could not untie the frozen knots of their pack loads. Meantime, the Bulgarian artillery had wrought havoc with the front line troops. The rocky ground, splintering on impact, intensified a hundredfold the killing-power of their high-explosive shells.

Notwithstanding the gallant efforts of the French on the left, contact could not be made with the Serbs, for already the Serbian Army, attacked by overwhelming numbers, had broken in two, and was fast in retreat across the Albanian Mountains, fighting splendid rearguard actions. After a short halt the French and

British Allied Forces were now confronted with the probability of an attack by the whole Bulgarian Army, which at the time could not have numbered less than four hundred thousand, also with the possibility of an attack in the rear by the then unfriendly Greek Army. So a withdrawal of the whole force on Salonica was decided upon. This was by no means an easy problem, for the same reasons that made the advance up country so difficult. The withdrawal was commenced by a retirement of the French on the left, and this had to be covered by the Irish Division, which held among the mountains a horseshoe line protecting the only road rearwards. When the main French forces had completed the first stage of their withdrawal, the Irish Division was faced by an attack of a vastly superior Bulgarian force. The main effort was made against the position held by the Battalion on Rocky Peak. The time had now arrived for the British force to commence its withdrawal, and after the most severe fighting, the Battalion withdrew with the remainder of the Irish Troops, and took up a new position on Crete Semene. Here a stand was made for twenty-four hours alongside some battalions of the 30th Brigade, and thereafter orders were received for a still further withdrawal to a position known as Causli Ridge. Some reorganisation was possible here, and the line was held for two days, when the Battalion was relieved by the advanced troops of the 22nd Division, which had recently landed at Salonica.

The Greek Frontier was now close at hand, and the Battalion withdrew to Doiran, where a halt was made for two days. The whole force was ordered to concentrate round Salonica, and entrained at Doiran Station, less the 31st Infantry Brigade, which was detailed to march, acting as a rearguard. The march to Salonica occupied a period of six days, during which time it rained continuously, and sleep and rest under such conditions in bleak open country were impossible. The actual marching of the rearguard Brigade was carried out across country in mud feet deep. Thus ended the Serbian Campaign, which in the opinion of competent judges had in this War been equalled only by the conditions of the first Winter in France and the first Summer in Mesopotamia.

Chapter IV.

MACEDONIA.

On arrival at Salonica on the 21st December the Battalion camped for two days on the outskirts of the town, and then marched to the village of Hortakoj, some ten kilos. from it. At this time it was believed that the attack begun by the Bulgarian Army would be developed into an onslaught on the town of Salonica and the Ægean Coast, the possession of which would have given to the Central Powers a submarine base from which they could harass our communications in the Mediterranean. This necessitated the construction of the outer defences of Salonica and the organisation of interior lines. Until the end of May the Battalion was engaged upon this work. The task was a difficult one, involving as it did in the sector occupied by the Brigade the cutting of trenches in almost solid rock. Acres of barbed wire were laid down, and roads were constructed changing the face of the whole country, and bringing wheeled traffic into valleys that from time immemorial had known only the peasant and his donkey. During these five months the Battalion recuperated effectually in the genial warmth of a Macedonian Spring from the hardships undergone on the sunbaked hills of Gallipoli and frost-bound heights of Serbia, and it was under the frowning heights of Mount Kotos, where once St. Paul preached to the Thessalonians that the Battalion celebrated its second Barrosa Day.

When late in June it became evident that the enemy did not intend advancing on Salonica, the Allied Army pushed forward. The British Forces moved into Northern Macedonia, the Battalion with the remainder of the 10th Division occupying heights overlooking the Struma Valley. Owing, however, to the varying situation, the Division became a mobile force, and was called upon to undertake long marches and counter-marches through roadless country, the entire transport being pack animals. In the first week of September the Battalion took up entrenched positions on the right bank of the River Struma, with the enemy in possession of the other bank. On the 10th September the 31st Brigade carried out a demonstration across the river against the strongly held villages Jenikoj, Bala and Zir, two companies of the Battalion taking an active part in the operation, whilst the other two were detached as a right flank guard.

The Brigade was complimented on the success of this reconnaissance in force, which proved a determining factor in the tactics of operations carried out soon after. The Battalion now reoccupied the River line, in a sector where the trenches were liable to be flooded at any moment, or the breastworks carried away by the river swollen with autumnal rains that fell among the Northern mountains. During the period of the occupation of the river line several very successful enterprises were carried out. These required the crossing of the strong-currented river, and men waded often with the water shoulder high, their only support being a rope secured to pickets on either side; on the opposite bank the patrols had to penetrate a thick undergrowth, and beyond, in most places, 'dense fields of high-growing mealies where enemy ambushes were often encountered.

In the second week of October the whole of the troops in the valley had crossed the river and driven the enemy to his prepared line on the foothills on the other side. The Battalion, with the remainder of the Brigade, was then withdrawn to Divisional Reserve in the neighbourhood of Baskoj.

On 30th October the Battalion, in conjunction with the 6th Battalion of the Regiment, was detailed to make a demonstration against the village of Prosenik. The primary object was to distract enemy attention from the main attack which was being carried out further on the left by the 28th Division against the strongly fortified locality of Barakli Dzuma. The village of Prosenik lay within easy range and direct observation of the numerous enemy batteries that guarded the entrance to the famous Rupel Pass. In this operation the Battalion demonstrated how well troops could protect themselves by disciplined and organised digging, for although the line entrenched lay in the open where there was not even the shelter of a blade of grass, they withstood an intense bombardment from the Rupel guns that lasted practically the whole of the daylight hours, and sustained remarkably few casualties.

This was the last operation in which the Battalion as originally constituted took part. On the 1st November orders were received to amalgamate with the 6th Battalion of the Regiment. It was intended that the amalgamation should be carried out whilst the two units were in reserve ; however, circumstances arose which necessitated both Battalions going into the line as separate units and amalgamating under exceptionally difficult circumstances when in the front line. The command of the newly organised 5th Battalion devolved upon Lieut.-Col. Greer. Except for domestic details, the history of the 6th Battalion was such as has been recorded here of its sister Battalion, the units having had equal share of the fortunes of war and the hardships of campaigning. The vacancy in the Brigade caused by the amalgamation was filled by the 2nd Battalion of the Regiment, under the command of Lt.-Col. H. P. Orpen Palmer.

Throughout the Summer and Autumn months the Battalion, in common with the other troops, suffered greatly from malarial fever, which is prevalent throughout Macedonia. The casualties from this alone were greater than those caused by the heaviest fighting. At one period in the month of September there were often twenty admissions a day to hospital, and this when the strength of the Battalion was less than four hundred. This fever developed in individuals with startling rapidity : a man might be at his post at 2 o'clock in the afternoon and at nightfall be carried away a victim. The malaria was of the recurrent type, a change of weather ofttimes causing a new attack. Ever afterwards, in no matter what theatre of war the Battalion was operating, this disease had to be reckoned with.

By the time the Battalion was again due for Divisional Reserve, Christmas had approached, and this season was spent in the neighbourhood of Orljak. Despite the difficulties of transport, owing to the appalling condition of the Seres Road, the only line of communication, a comparatively sumptuous dinner was provided. During the winter months, whenever the Battalion was not in the line, sports of all kinds were engaged in. The chief feature was a Brigade Group Football League. Eighteen matches in all were played by the Regimental Team, only one being lost and one drawn, and the Battalion came out easy winners. The Officers' Rugby Team had also a good season, never losing a game.

The Winter and Spring were passed in and out of the line in normal reliefs. During the periods in the line the Battalion made patrol actions and raids a nightly business, and, developing this type of warfare to suit local conditions, brought it to a fine art. In this theatre of war the opposing lines were sometimes several thousand yards apart, and this spacious " No Man's Land " was the happy hunting ground of subalterns, who with their handful of men went forth nightly to a combat of wit and arms with the Bulgar, a pastmaster of woodcraft. Here, if anywhere in the War, the spirit of adventure had scope and the sporting instincts had play, for the modern mechanism of scientific manslaughter was eliminated ; men were pitted against men, and the sharpest wit and strongest arm won the day. So wholeheartedly did the Battalion enter into the spirit of this game that they always had complete mastery of their sector of " No Man's Land," often surprising the enemy outposts, but never once being worsted themselves.

On the approach of Summer it was decided to evacuate the valley, said to be the second most unhealthy place in Europe. Bridgeheads and a line of posts were established to hold the River Line. From May to August was spent alternately either on the foothills overlooking the Struma Valley, with one company on the River Line in the vicinity of Cuckoo Bridge, or on the higher hills behind, some 2,000 feet above the river at Four Trees.

During these Summer months the greatest enemy was the mosquito, and a most elaborate paraphernalia of warfare was developed to deal with it. Men dared not leave any part of their bodies uncovered : netted masks were provided for the head and neck, stout fabric gloves for the hands, and extension flaps to the shorts for knee covering. When, however, work was to be done that demanded the fullest use of the senses, masks could not be worn ; and an evil-smelling ointment, " Paraquit," had to be smeared over the face. But, notwithstanding all these precautions, the mosquito usually had its way, and wherever cloth or net touched the skin the victim found himself stung.

On the 21st May Lt.-Col. F. A. Greer was appointed Brigadier-General to command the 30th Infantry Brigade, having three months previously commanded the 84th Brigade, and demonstrated his excellent qualities as a commander. Major F. W. E. Johnson was appointed Lieutenant-Colonel, and assumed command of the

Battalion. During the Summer months it was possible to indulge in a good deal of sport, and a Brigade Sports Meeting was held, in which the Battalion demonstrated its already proved superiority, the 2nd Battalion being runners-up.

In September rumours of a probable move to another theatre of war became rife. Eventually the Irish troops were relieved by the 28th Division, and, after the usual vicissitudes that attend troops on the move, found themselves sailing to Egypt, *en route* for Palestine.

This ended two years of warfare in the Balkans, to the memory chiefly composed of hardship, disease and ennui, where touch with civilisation was all but lost, for the beloved mail came only once in three weeks, and often, " owing to enemy action at sea," came not at all, and the often promised, but never realised, leave to " Blighty " loomed large, only in dreamland.

Chapter V.

PALESTINE.

The voyage to Alexandria lasted three days, during the daylight hours of one of which the ship put into Skyros, a sunny island of the Ægean Archipelago, to seek the protection of its excellent harbourage from the enemy submarines which infested this danger zone. On the 25th the Battalion disembarked at Alexandria and entrained for Ismalia, a pleasant town on the banks of the Suez Canal. Its week's stay here was regarded by all in the nature of a holiday, as this was the first touch of civilisation that the Battalion had enjoyed for over two years. The next move was along the banks of the Canal, three days' route march, to Kantara, the base of the Palestine Forces. After two days the unit entrained and crossed the Sinai Desert to Rafa, where a period of intensive training under desert conditions was engaged in. Here Officers and N.C.O's. learned the art of keeping direction by reading of stars, and men were schooled in the intricacies of transport by camels.

The Palestine Campaign of the Winter, 1917-1918, was now about to begin. At this time the enemy line stretched from the sea eastwards through Gaza across desert country to Beersheba, where his left flank was protected by a vast expanse of uninhabitable and waterless country. The task assigned to the Irish troops, in which the Battalion took a prominent part, was the piercing of this line midway between the towns of Gaza and Beersheba.

After about three weeks' stay at Rafa, the Battalion, with the remainder of the 10th Division, advanced in two night marches to Shellal, some four kilometres south of the enemy line; here in the Wadi Ghuzze it took cover for two days from enemy aircraft, while it awaited the development of the forthcoming attack. Thereafter, in two forced marches, plodding in inches deep of soft sand, the Battalion moved further eastwards and took over the outpost line from the troops of the 53rd Division on the heights overlooking

Wadi Hanafish. On the 2nd November, the same day as the outposts were taken over, the Battalion advanced the line to the neighbourhood of Irgeig, six miles West of Beersheba.

At this time, and particularly in this district, the scarcity of water was very acute, the allowance being one quart per head per day for all purposes, and even this meagre allowance was brackish in taste, and had to be carried by camels from wells fourteen or fifteen miles in the rear. Suffering from dearth of water was not confined to men alone, for the Regimental Transport, consisting entirely of camels and pack mules, had their full share of the hardships, being on one occasion seventy-three hours without water. Since Gallipoli this was the severest test of the discipline and morale of the Battalion, and never better or more cheerfully by any troops was test endured.

The attack on Beersheba and the envelopment of the enemy's left flank had now begun, and, coincidently with this operation, the Battalion, with the remainder of the 31st Brigade, moved through Irgeig on the night of the 5th November to its place of assembly preparatory to an attack on the following day. On 6th November the objective allotted to the 31st Brigade was the Rushdi System, a network of well constructed and strongly wired trenches.

The order to attack was not received till 11 a.m., but when once started it went with such a swing that the artillery found it impossible to keep pace with it. The 5th and 2nd Battalions of the Regiment, side by side, led the attack on the Brigade Sector, the units vying with one another in rapidity of advance. This was the first occasion on which these two Battalions of Royal Irish Fusiliers had taken the field together in an attack ; the sight of the two Battalions as they crossed the flat open plain through a dense artillery barrage, without pause or falter, will not be forgotten by those who were witnesses of it.

In an almost incredibly short space of time this strong position was in our hands, and it was only with the greatest difficulty that the men could be restrained from launching a further attack on the retiring enemy, but, owing to the fact that a definite objective had been laid down, this impetuosity had to be curbed.

With the capture of this position very large quantities of material of all sorts fell into our hands, amongst other things two field kitchens containing the complete dinner of a Turkish battalion boiling hot, as they had left it in their hasty retirement. During the evening and night the position was consolidated.

In the early hours of the 7th orders were received by the Brigade for the capture of the Hareira Tepe Redoubt, a high eminence some 2,000 yards distant, and said to have been the strongest position in Southern Palestine. The Turks considered it almost impregnable, defended as it was by heavy trench mortars and a very large number of machine guns, in addition to artillery. The task of reducing this stronghold was assigned within the Brigade to the 2nd Battalion and two companies of the 5th Battalion, the whole under the command of Lt.-Col. Orpen Palmer, D.S.O. In spite of rather heavy casualties the entire position was, after three hours' very severe fighting, taken by assault. During the attack an out-of-the-way incident occurred: a battery of howitzers, urgently and unexpectedly called for, whose horses were watering at wells seven miles distant, were brought into action at the gallop by mules of the Regimental Transport.

There was another incident, small in its way, but showing something of the spirit of the men. One platoon in the act of serving out tea, received the order to advance; nothing daunted, they carried their dixie until such time as the tea was cool enough to drink, when, under comparatively heavy machine gun fire, each man filled his mess tin as opportunity occurred and continued the attack.

After the capture of this formidable redoubt the remaining companies of the Battalion pushed through and formed an outpost line, the two companies which had made the attack being in support, and the 2nd Battalion of the Regiment in reserve. Very little opposition was met, and the following morning it was discovered that the Turks had fled. Thus ended this phase of the operations.

By now the enemy had been driven from the general Gaza-Beersheba line, closely pursued by cavalry and the 21st Corps. The 20th Corps, which had endured much fighting, marching and counter-marching, to say nothing of privation and thirst in the desert, was withdrawn to the vicinity of railhead where rations and water could more easily be obtained. The Battalion, as part of this Corps, pegged down its bivouacs in the vicinity of Karm, where for three days it lived in a thick low-lying cloud of dust raised by a " Khamseen " wind. Dysentery and diarrhœa were rife in this district, and it was with no regrets that the Battalion marched westwards across the desert to Belah, near the coast, about three miles south of Gaza.

In about a week's time the communications up-country had been improved and organised to such an extent that more troops could be despatched in pursuit of the Turks. The Irish Troops accordingly, about the end of November, marched northwards through the Land of Goschen and by way of the Valley of Ajalon to the relief of the 52nd (Scottish Division), which had had many severe engagements amongst the Judean Hills. The Battalion encountered the enemy in the vicinity of Beit-ur-el-Tahta, the Biblical Lower Beth-Horon, the very ground where it is told Joshua slew the five kings of the Philistines. The enemy in this neighbourhood occupied commanding positions on the heights of Kareina and on Foka. At this place the Battalion was about ten miles westward of Jerusalem, and it was decided that its position should be made the pivotal point for the attack on the City. On 9th December the attack was launched and Jerusalem enveloped, the whole right flank of the Army swinging round on the defensive position held by the Battalion.

Christmas found the Battalion in Divisional Reserve, and, as usual, road-making day and night. The worst possible Christmas was passed : rain came down in torrents, and in the Wadi, where the Battalion was bivouaced, a rushing stream came suddenly into being, sweeping shelters, equipments and stores in its flood. There was no mail to cheer, and the troops, on account of their distance in advance of railhead and the inaccessibility of their positions, were living on quarter rations. To make matters worse, on Christmas Eve, all had to stand in readiness for action at a moment's notice, for the enemy, hoping to catch the British troops merrymaking, had prepared a counter-attack on a large scale for the re-capture of Jerusalem. This scheme, however, it afterwards transpired, had to be abandoned on this night, owing to the torrential rains.

The enemy attack was launched in great strength two days later directly east and north of the City. Simultaneously the Irish Troops were called upon to make a counter-attack which had for its aim the piercing of the enemy's line and the cutting at

Ram-Allah of communications, between this attacking army and the base at Nablus. This movement was carried out eastwards across the enemy's front to a depth of four miles over most precipitous country, eventually reaching the vicinity of Ram-Allah (a day's journey north of Jerusalem). The operations as carried out by the Battalion, in conjunction with other troops of the 31st Brigade resulted in the capture of the commanding heights known as Kareina, Three Tree Ridge, Hog's Back, Ain Jeirut, Kefr Shyan, Ain Sabieh, and were completed in the consolidation of a high hill known as El Muntar. These heights form the ridge that overlooks from the north and west the Wadi Sunt, known Biblically as the Valley of Elah, the scene of the historic encounter between David and Goliath. To say that this country was difficult for campaigning is to convey little idea of it. It was a chaotic welter of hills intersected by deep wadis, the sides of which were precipitous and terraced, as is usual in Judea. The terraces were a great hindrance to progress, as they were almost always from six to ten feet high, and so broke any continuity of advance in a direct line. These hills were held by machine gun nests, often cunningly concealed in caves with infantry posts in support. Each and every one of these posts had to be ferretted out for often, so open was the warfare, a post would remain silent until the first advancing troops had passed. Had it not been for the hardness and fitness of the men, the notable triumph gained by the Irish Troops in carrying out their programme to scheduled time would have been well-nigh impossible. The rapidity of their advance completed the discomfiture of the Turks, who, instead of getting the Holy City into their grasp by one great coup had, on account of the menace to their communications to begin a hasty withdrawal.

It was now the end of the first week of January, 1918, and a pause had to be made, owing to the entire absence of roads in the territory just captured. For the next three weeks the Battalion, with other troops of the Brigade, was employed in making what will doubtless go down to posterity as the Irish Road, which joins the Jerusalem-Nablus Road near Ram-Allah to the Coastal Plain, running through numerous wadis in the Judean Hill system, and passing Ain Arik, the Archi of the Bible.

At the conclusion of this period of road-making, the Battalion relieved the Royal Munster Fusiliers in their outpost line, taking over the hills of Meiderus, Harasheh, and Shiek Aisa. Harasheh, the highest point in the neighbourhood, made a splendid observation post overlooking the enemy's territory. From here one could see to the south the tumultous mass of hills which had already been captured, prominent among them being El Gib and Neby Samuel ; to the north, giving earnest of the fighting that lay in store, the Mountains of Ephraim in the foreground, and in the distance Mount Carmel, the Hills of Lebanon and Mount Tabor. Westwards there was a far different picture, the low-lying Coastal Plain with its rich orange groves and the minarets of Jaffa and Ludd gleaming white amongst the dark foliage of the olive trees. Fringing it lay the blue Mediterranean, sparkling in the sunlight.

While holding these outposts many distinguished visitors, including the Commander-in-Chief, Sir Edmund Allenby, and General Smuts, visited the Battalion's area.

From the outpost line it became necessary to make a thorough reconnaissance preparatory to the next advance, and in this connection the Battalion Scouts and Patrols did excellent work, very often penetrating the enemy's outposts. Twenty-eight days were spent in the outpost zone, the first fortnight being raw, winterish weather with heavy rains. On the 4th March the Battalion was withdrawn for a few days' rest prior to taking part in the next phase of the general advance.

Barrosa Day found the Battalion getting ready for action. The general plan of the forthcoming operations was an attack astride the Nablus-Jerusalem Road by the 20th Corps, the 10th Irish Division being on the left flank. The 74th Division was on the right of the 10th Division, and in the centre of the Corps. The positions to be attacked consisted of a series of strongly held ridges, intersected by great wadis, or ravines, and these ridges extended for miles across country and at points were over 3,000 feet high.

At dusk on the evening of the 8th the Battalion moved to its place of assembly at Bir-ez-Zeit. At dawn on the morning of the 9th the general attack commenced. Fog hampered the initial operations and rendered the keeping of direction exceedingly difficult. Within the Brigade Sector the two Battalions of the Regiment again took the field side by side, the 5th Battalion being the right of the Division. The task allotted to the Battalion was the capture in succession of Zeitoun, Ras-el-Tarfii, and Attara

Ridges, including Attara village. As soon as the fog cleared the attack was launched, and in a very short space of time the first objective, Zeitoun Ridge, had been made good. The advance continued without a pause, and by 10.0 a.m. the second objective, Ras-el-Tarfii, had been stormed and captured, despite the heavy enemy barrage. Here a slight halt was necessary to enable the Division on the right to come into line, and the Battalion was able to witness the splendid attack on and capture of that formidable stronghold Sheik Kalrawany and Hill 2791 by the 2nd Battalion of the Regiment. During this pause valuable work was done by Lewis Gunners in harrassing the retreating enemy, and in bringing flanking fire to bear to assist the battalions on the right and left, Attara Village and Ridge were taken before noon, by which time all enemy batteries were in full play on the captured ground. It now became necessary to form a defensive flank on the right, for the troops on the flank had still much ground to make good, and the position was consolidated by the hasty construction of small sangar posts, as trenches were out of the question on account of the rocky nature of the ground.

Reconnaissance showed that the carrying out of the following day's programme was a task of no small difficulty. In front ran the Wadi El-Gib, one of the deepest and largest ravines in Palestine. It was overlooked on the enemy side by an immense ridge, three outstanding features of which were Hills K3, K4, and K12,* all of which averaged 3,000 feet.

The passage of this wadi was a matter of extreme difficulty, and during the afternoon patrols were sent out to discover the best lines of descent, the possible wadi crossings, and the lines of ascent to the hills opposite. In the evening, just before dusk, orders were received to send one company across this wadi to occupy Hill K4, about the enemy occupation of which there was some doubt. When the company had arrived half way down the slope the enemy opened a heavy machine gun fire from all three hills opposite. Ignoring this, the company continued until the wadi bed was reached. By this time, owing to the darkness and to the broken nature of the ground, in the descent two platoons unfortunately became detached and lost touch. Notwithstanding, the other two

---

* These Hills being nameless take their designations from the map squares in which they were situated.

platoons commenced the ascent of Hill K4, which was now definitely known to be occupied. As soon as the two platoons came in close contact with the enemy sangars, a heavy fire from all infantry arms, rifles, machine guns and trench mortars was opened on them, and it became evident that the position was held in too great strength to admit of being captured by such a small force. However, the Commander on the spot decided not to withdraw, but to hold on to the footing gained. Here this mere handful of men was two and a half thousand yards in advance of the main line of troops. It was without telephonic communication on account of the distance of objective, and the nearest supporting troops, owing to the darkness and the precipitous nature of the ground, could not render assistance. Flashes from an electric lamp right under the enemy's nose spoke out of the darkness, and told of the precarious position occupied. During the whole night the enemy was unceasing in his efforts to dislodge these intruders. Repeatedly he sent forward patrols and snipers, and when these failed he drenched the position with rifle and trench mortar bombs. The little band, however, held on and busied itself in strengthening its position for all-round defence. Meantime the flash lamp, sniped at all the while, told from time to time the situation.

At dawn it was decided that the party should make another attempt to rush the enemy sangars and silence his machine guns. An advance of two hundred yards was made in the face of the concentrated fire of five machine guns, but, owing to the number of casualties sustained, the attempt had to be given up. The tenacity of this little force, maintaining its position throughout the long hours of darkness, and its gallant attempt at dawn was a performance worthy of the best traditions of the Regiment.

For the final capture of the position it was decided soon after daylight to reinforce the two platoons that had held on all night, by two companies of the Battalion and one company of the 5th R. Inniskilling Fusiliers. One of these was the supporting company that had been across the wadi all night on the right flank of the two platoons on the hill. The other company of the Battalion and the company of Inniskillings had to descend into the wadi in broad daylight under severe artillery fire, and through a barrage laid down by seven or eight machine guns firing frontally from Hill K4, and very obliquely from Hills K3 and K2. Nevertheless, the men held on their course, rushing down the hillside, keeping their footing in a most wonderful fashion, leaping from terrace to terrace, and performing feats that would in cold blood have appeared impossible to men equipped as they were.

The ascent of Hill K4 was made under the enfilade fire of two machine guns from K12; but ultimately the position of assault was reached in sufficient numbers to make a charge possible. Possible, but not too promising, for the enemy breastworks were fully two hundred yards off, topping a slope where the ground rose at about an angle of forty-five degrees, and over which their field of fire was perfect. The men, however, could not be restrained, and with a mighty shout of " FAUGH-A-BALLAGH " they went over the top to the charge. As the troops assaulted they were enfiladed by machine guns, one gun even taking them in the rear, and were subjected to a heavy frontal fire until the foremost of them were within forty yards of the enemy breastworks and emplacements. The charge was crowned with success, and the defending garrison which had held on so pluckily till the end, surrendered with its rifles, machine guns and bombs.

On the fall of Hill K4, Hill K12 was evacuated, and Hill K3 fell to the troops on the left as a matter of course.

A pause was now necessary to get up supplies and ammunition, and to allow the artillery time to get into position for a further advance. The front edge of Hill K4 was lightly held by a line of observation posts, which were all day subjected to an intense bombardment and heavy machine gun fire. About 4 p.m. orders were received for the further advance, and two companies of the Battalion once more took up the running, and again, in the face of very heavy fire, stormed the Village of Jiljilia (the ancient Gilgal), capturing the heights on which it stood and the ridge to the east.

During all this advance the 31st Machine Gun Company rendered the greatest assistance by their admirably directed machine gun fire. The capture of Jiljilia placed all the objectives allotted for the operations in our hands, and it is worthy of record that the Brigade was the only one in the Army to secure all its objectives in the specified time.

Once again a halt was ordered, not through inability to pursue the Turk, but by the absolute necessity for making roads in this trackless country. There was another spell of road-making, though it fell to the lot of the Battalion to maintain the outpost line for the greater portion of this period. After a fortnight in the line the Battalion was drawn into reserve, but shortly again took up the task of road-making, and continued thus for ten days.

At the end of this period orders were received for the Brigade to move into support to the 75th Division, who were about to attack a portion of the enemy's line. In the event of this attack being successful the Brigade was to pass through the 75th Division, forming a flying column to harass the retreating enemy. With this object all kit and equipment was reduced to the lowest minimum, the entire transport consisting of pack animals carrying ammunition and rations. Through a change in plan these operations did not materialise. At this time happenings in France were of such a serious nature that with the decision to concentrate all available white troops on the Western Front, the Battalion, with the greater number of units in the Irish Division, were transferred to France. The Battalion's place in the 31st Brigade was taken by an Indian battalion, namely, the 74th Punjabis, and orders were received to march to railhead at Ludd to entrain for Kantara.

Whilst at Kantara the Battalion was re-equipped—a work of no little difficulty—on the European scale. After about a fortnight at Kantara, the Battalion embarked on board the " Huntspill " at Port Said, in company with the 2nd Battalion Loyal North Lancashire Regiment, and sailed for France on 18th May.

CHAPTER VI.

FRANCE.

Marseilles was reached on 27th May, and after four days the Battalion entrained for Aire, in Northern France. The journey occupied four days, and the usual discomforts were endured.

On arrival at Aire the Battalion marched to the little village of Manqueville, where it enjoyed the luxury of billets and bade farewell to the bivouac, which had for three years, summer and winter, been its sole shelter. Here it was attached to the reorganised 14th Division, and was allotted to the Merville Sector. The excessive cold and damp of the West coming hard upon a long spell in the Near East before the troops had been fully acclimatised, gave rise to a serious outbreak of malaria. Several hundred men had to be evacuated to hospital in a space of ten days, and this at a period when in this particular zone of operations every rifle counted. As a result of this depletion it seemed likely that the Battalion would be broken up to supply drafts to local units. However, the Corps Commander, Lieut.-General Peyton, seeing that this was a Battalion still very largely composed of men of the First Hundred Thousand, and of men of the pre-war Regular Army, all veteran soldiers with three years and more continuous service in the field, brimful of *esprit de corps*, and retaining their old smartness and appearance, reported against this, preferring that the unit be kept intact for the more strenuous days ahead. As a result of this, the Battalion was moved to milder regions further South, and was embodied in the 30th Division. Ultimately the unit was transferred to the reorganised 66th Division, becoming part of the Army of Manœuvre. After an inspection of all infantry units of the 66th Division, which was composed of some of the finest units from Eastern theatres, the G.O.C., Major-General Bethell, awarded premier honours to the Battalion, placing it at the top of the list for general efficiency and smartness. On 7th August the military situation permitted, and the Battalion for the first time was enabled to celebrate, with the time-honoured Sports Meeting, the anniversary of its landing at Suvla.

By the middle of August the great Allied counter offensive had been made along the whole front with such success that all ranks in the Battalion were granted a well-earned furlough. The vast majority had not had the opportunity to visit their homes since Christmas, 1914, and they now proceeded to the United Kingdom in batches of two and three hundred at a time.

Scarcely had the men returned from leave when the Battalion was transferred to still another Division, this time the 16th, which had just been reorganised. On joining this formation about the end of August the unit found itself in the La Bassee Sector, a region well known to most fighting men in France. Here the line had remained almost stationary for four years. It was the only sector where the original trenches and underground tunnels were still in use, and on account of their long occupation they had become infested with rats and vermin. By the first week in October, however, the line had been advanced, and the famous landmarks, the Hohenzollern Redoubt and the La Bassee Leave Train, had been left behind. Whilst holding the ruins that once formed the Village of Auchy the Battalion was subjected to its heaviest gas bombardment, but owing to the high standard of gas discipline obtaining the casualties were extraordinarily few. By this time the rigidity of the purely trench warfare had been broken, and the Battalion, which had won from the enemy so much ground in Macedonia and Palestine, had the opportunity of making its presence felt in France. Ample scope for offensive patrols and minor operations was found ; one platoon, for instance, in a raid launched in broad daylight, succeeded in cutting off an enemy post and capturing its two machine guns.

By the middle of October a further advance had been made across the La Bassee-Haute Deule Canal, and open warfare began.

During a pause in this advance, at a time when the Battalion was in Divisional Reserve at a village called Ennevelin, the civil population, to commemorate its deliverance from the enemy, held a thanksgiving service, to which the Battalion was invited. As a result of the good feeling existing between the inhabitants and the Regiment, it was felt that it would be very fitting that the unit should commemorate its stay there by subscribing to replace the Church bell, stolen by the enemy. The subscription was very liberally contributed to by all ranks, and it was formally presented to the Maire in the name of the Battalion, and, at the request of the Curé, the name " MARIE-GEORGES "—in honour of Their Majesties, was chosen for the bell. A tablet also is to be erected in the Church bearing the following inscription :—" PRESENTED BY THE 5TH SERVICE BATTALION OF THE ROYAL IRISH FUSILIERS AS A TOKEN OF THEIR ESTEEM AND REGARD FOR THE FRENCH NATION."

In the next phase the Battalion was called upon to make a reconnaissance of the River Scheldt, south-west of Antoing; this was carried out under a very heavy bombardment. Active patrol work was done during a period of heavy winter rain, and at 4.0 a.m. on 8th November the Battalion was able to report that the enemy was preparing a withdrawal, this being the first intimation at Army Headquarters. Fighting Patrols moved out immediately, in spite of all difficulties, and by dusk the same evening occupied the west bank of the Scheldt, with the enemy in dominating machine-gun positions on the opposite bank, on the top of a neighbouring fosse and on the roofs of houses.

On the following day the crossing of the river was carried out without opposition, and on the 10th November the Battalion moved into Antoing.

The news of the signing of the Armistice was received on the 11th, on which day the Battalion was paraded before the Brigade Commander, Brigadier-General R. N. Bray, D.S.O., who expressed his very great appreciation of the work done by the unit in France, and the cheerfulness displayed by all ranks under very great difficulties.

* * *

Thus ended the Battalion's efforts in the

GREAT WAR.

This little book would be incomplete without a word of thanks to those at home who have worked so faithfully and unremittingly these four years to provide comforts of all kinds for the men while overseas. The regular receipt of large numbers of gifts showed that the Battalion, in its distant theatres of war, had still a warm corner in the hearts of many at home, and this proved a great factor in the maintenance of the splendid morale which has always existed in the unit.

It was evident to all in the Battalion that the mere labour of organisation, the collecting and packing, to say nothing of the actual making of the comforts to satisfy the needs of some eight or nine hundred men, must have been enormous.

The sincerest thanks of all ranks are due in the first place

- To MRS. EVANS JOHNSON, Thomastown ;
- To the RELATIVES OF THE OFFICERS AND FRIENDS OF THE BATTALION ;
- To MR. DELMAGE TRIMBLE, of the " Armagh Guardian"
- To the RESIDENTS OF ARMAGH AND CAVAN ;
- To the IRISH WOMEN'S ASSOCIATION ;
- To the ULSTER WOMEN'S ASSOCIATION ;
- To QUEEN MARY'S NEEDLEWORK GUILD ; and
- To the CONTRIBUTORS TO QUEEN ALEXANDRA'S FIELD FORCE FUND.

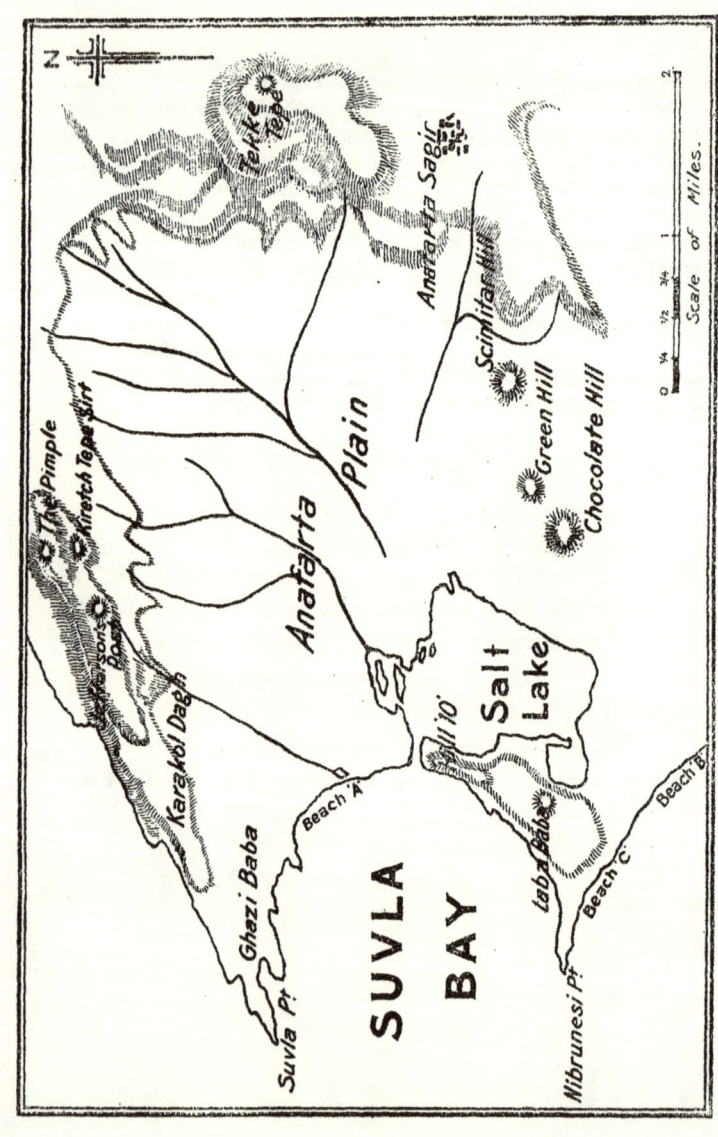

Officers who Embarked with the Battalion for Active Service in 1915.

Lieut.-Colonel.

M. J. W. PIKE.

Majors.

F. W. E. JOHNSON.
W. F. C. GARSTIN.

Captains.

E. M. McILWAINE.	A. W. SCOTT-SKIRVING.
H. G. WHYTE.	J. A. D. DEMPSEY.
G. G. DUGGAN.	W. J. HARTLEY.

Lieutenants.	*2nd Lieutenants.*
W. A. BEATTIE.	C. CROSLEY.
J. B. ATKINSON.	F. A. NEWELL.
A. R. TUDOR CRAIG.	D. T. FIGGIS.
C. F. N. HARRIS.	P. H. D. DEMPSEY.
R. V. MURRAY.	J. L. CHALMERS.
J. A. BLOOD.	E. A. EVANSON.
C. A. MURRAY.	J. L. BENNETT.
H. S. C. PANTON.	M. B. GRAHAM.
L. C. FITZGERALD.	G. M. KIDD.

Adjutant.

CAPT. P. E. KELLY.

Quartermaster.

LIEUT. J. CAMPBELL.

Officers Serving on Amalgamation, 2nd Nov., 1916.

Lieut.-Colonel.
*F. A. GREER.

Major.
*F. W. E. JOHNSON.

Captains.

*A. R. TUDOR-CRAIG, M.C.
*P. C. TUDOR-CRAIG.
*J. A. BLOOD.
J. MANNING.
*A. G. PORTER, M.C.
*W. A. BEATTIE.
*G. M. KIDD, M.C.

Lieutenants.   *2nd Lieutenants.*

*C. A. MURRAY.
*G. G. HIGGINS.
*L. C. FITZGERALD.
*A. V. McNEILL.
*D. T. FIGGIS.
W. F. DICKSON.
*H. E. SHERRARD.
A. E. BROWNE.
T. O. HOWIE.
W. A. STRANGE.
R. McEWAN.
R. J. STRANGER.
R. BRENNAN, M.C.
E. J. ECCLES.
G. E. SEBRIGHT.
L. R. MUIRHEAD.
*C. BARTON.
P. E. H. HAIGH.
A. V. AMES.
J. TATE.
E. S. L. TEES.
J. S. THOMPSON.
W. T. HALL.

Adjutant.
LIEUT. E. L. BANFIELD.

Quartermaster.
*LIEUT. J. CAMPBELL.

* *Original Officers of either 5th or 6th Battalions.*

Officers Serving on Armistice Day.

Lieut.-Colonel.
*F. W. E. JOHNSON, D.S.O.

Majors.
B. R. FRENCH, D.S.O.
*H. S. SWEETING.

Captains.

*W. A. BEATTIE, M.C.	G. C. KIRKLAND.
*D. T. FIGGIS.	*H. E. SHERRARD.
R. McEWAN, M.C.	E. M. SMITH.
*G. H. GALLOGLY.	

Lieutenants.	*2nd Lieutenants.*
F. S. SIMPSON.	J. H. DUNCAN.
A. V. AMES.	A. W. CARR.
A. E. BROWNE.	W. L. DIX.
R. J. STRANGER, M.C.	H. A. J. BERRY.
L. R. MUIRHEAD.	T. J. GALLAGHER.
E. J. ECCLES.	T. E. DILNOT.
H. B. REYNELL.	J. THORNTON.
T. GERAGHTY, M.C.	J. CARROLL, M.C., M.S.M.
T. H. CORRIGAN.	L. WARD, D.C.M.
P. I. R. SANDILANDS.	P. J. T. CATER.
R. V. JACKSON.	J. H. DOLAN.

Adjutant.
CAPT. W. F. DICKSON.

Quartermaster.
*CAPT. J. CAMPBELL.

* *Original Officers of either 5th or 6th Battalions*

Alphabetical List

OF

Officers who have Served with the Battalion

Lieut.-Colonels.

FURNELL, M. J.
ROOKE, G. H. J. (Leinster Regt.)

Majors.

ADAMS, G. S. C. (R. W. Surrey Regt.)
GORDON, J. G.

Captains.

GRUNE, E. S. C. (Bedford Regt.)
McVEAGH, F. A. (4th Bn.)
ORLEBAR, R. A. B. (Bedford Regt.)
*OLIVER, A. F.
STEWART, W., *M.C.* (3rd Bn.)
VERNON, H. A. (4th Bn.)

Lieutenants.

CREIGHTON, J. L.	McCULLAGH, T.
ESPIE, T. F.	PATTERSON, J. L.
KING, C. H. (4th Bn.)	*SMITH, A. MAUNSELL.
MOORE, W. M.	STEVENTON, R. W. (4th Bn.)
MAHONEY, M. F. J. R.	SORGE, R. P.
MARCHANT, L. ALLMAN.	VERDON, E. H.
MACKIE, C. B. (Royal Scots).	

* Original Members of 5th Battalion.

2nd Lieutenants.

Arlott, M. J.	James, A. A. (Conn. Rang.)
Arnott, T.	King, F. G. W. (S. Staffs).
Brownlee, F.	Lenny, W. (,,)
Beevor, R. B.	Lee, W. (,,)
Cullen, R. N.	*Maxwell, R.
Carr, A. W.	*Madden, P. J.
Darragh, C. Q.	Moss, H. W.
Green, F.	McFarland, F. J. E., M.C.
Hourihane, G. O'B.	Stewart, I. F.
Healy, B. E. L.	Thunder, A. E.

Original Members of 5th Battalion.

www.ingramcontent.com/pod-product-compliance
Lightning Source LLC
Chambersburg PA
CBHW051719040426
42446CB00008B/963